CHRISTIAN POETRY

4 US ALL

CHRISTIAN POETRY

4 US ALL

M. ROBERTS

XULON PRESS

Xulon Press
2301 Lucien Way #415
Maitland, FL 32751
407.339.4217
www.xulonpress.com

© 2020 by Michael Roberts

All rights reserved solely by the author. The author guarantees all contents are original and do not infringe upon the legal rights of any other person or work. No part of this book may be reproduced in any form without the permission of the author. The views expressed in this book are not necessarily those of the publisher.

Unless otherwise indicated, Scripture quotations taken from the Holy Bible, New International Version (NIV). Copyright © 1973, 1978, 1984, 2011 by Biblica, Inc.™. Used by permission. All rights reserved.

Printed in the United States of America.

Paperback ISBN-13: 978-1-6312-9605-5

Ebook ISBN-13: 978-1-6312-9606-2

TABLE OF CONTENTS

This is The Test................................. 1
I did not know.................................. 2
The Struggle For Happiness 3
Let it Go....................................... 4
L I F E 5
It's a Beautiful Thing 6
The Journey 7
I've Got God 8
For the Children 9
Dear God,...................................... 10
The Apology 11
Dear anyone,................................... 12
Forgiveness 13
A True Look at the Gifts......................... 14
A 'New Day.................................... 15
A question?................................... 16
Question 17
A Slow Descent................................ 18
The Revocation of God's Promise 19
Blessed,...................................... 20

Gluttony	21
<u>Hate</u> is ugly in any color!.	22
AGAIN	23
I Quit!	24
Want for What?	25
Red Rose distractions	26
My life is good, my life is great.	27
True Richness	28
Another Burdensome Task!	29
<u>The Apology</u>, as Legal Document	30
The Pledge of Allegiance	31
Declaration of Independence.	32
Poor Souls	33
Knowing	34
There is no excuse	35
The time	36
We the Christians	37
I will not die!!!	38
Not dead yet	39

THIS IS THE TEST.

This is the Test.
Not to be confused with problems within
this finite life in the flesh.
A fact of the matter is
a good 100-year life is
equal to zero years in eternity.
This is the Test.
Where & how do you and your family
wish to spend eternity?
We the Christians hope and pray that
You will accept salvation & pursue Jesus Christ
then the answer to the question is
Heaven it will be.

I DID NOT KNOW

I had a problem I could not fix.
I tried, I tried, & I tried
only making the problem worse.
I then prayed to a God I didn't believe in.

"God if you are real, please help I can't fix this."
A short time later the impossible problem was fixed.
I looked to the skies and said, "thank you"
and went back to my old ways.

Later another unfixable problem occurred.
I then prayed to a God I did not know.
A short time later the problem was fixed.
This time I had to get to know this
God that answered prayers

To the God I did not know
THANK YOU, Jesus Christ,
for everything you do.

THE STRUGGLE FOR HAPPINESS

A struggle for happiness
where little may be found
A struggle for happiness
where drugs, adultery, & trespass
may run freely without bounds,
causing pain, misery, and suffering,
for all around.

Struggling as I did, suffering through my plight
the only true happiness I found
came after accepting Jesus Christ as my lord and savior,
repenting for my sins,
& started living
to the best of my ability,
Christ-like.

LET IT GO…

Because of the horrors in my life that happened
I allowed my un-forgivingness to keep me trapped in.
I was given the privilege to let go and Let God
or continue with my own self-tormenting ride.
Note to self:
do not EVER forget Pride
as it may linger inside;
trying to revoke the privilege
that God so graciously did provide.

LIFE

My life is like a small boat on the beautiful ocean.
I never know what the weather will be:
Sometimes cloudy, sometimes sunny
and sometimes violently stormy.
While I know what my plans are,
I do not know what God's plans will be.
I want to make it to the beautiful island
with the beautiful flowers and the beautiful trees
but if I do not make it where I plan
I will know not to worry
because, God
is always with me.

IT'S A BEAUTIFUL THING

It's a beautiful thing
which he hath done for us:
He sent his only begotten Son
to suffer and die on the cross for us.
While this really does sound extremely horrifying,
the fact of the matter is
to us it is truly glorifying.
Now, with repentance
we can wash away all of our sins
because of this wonderful thing
that our God has done for us.

THE JOURNEY

Before I walked with him,
He walked with me.
Thankfully, I was given
the privilege to accept Jesus Christ
as my Lord and Savior
I now know,
when I am done with this body
I will continue the journey

                                        For:
                                        in Christ Heaven it
                                        shall be!!!

I'VE GOT GOD

You can beat me; you can imprison me;
you can lie about the way I live,
but you cannot destroy me:
I've got God

You can take away my house; you can take away my car;
you can even un-employ me,
and think I won't get far.
You cannot even discourage me
I've got God

You will see I have serenity through all of my strife;
you will see I have contentment
through all of my life;
You cannot even influence me,
and you know why —
because I've got God
and he is the center of my life.

FOR THE CHILDREN

If you have children and you want them to be happy
Know this, Jesus Christ my Lord and Savior
loves you and wants you to be happy too.
If you have children and you want them to be happy.
It is your responsibility to show them how.
Further, if you have children and want them to be happy.
We must realize, whatever problems were facing today
it could be worse and probably has been.
So, it is now our responsibility
to be happy and show them how.

Ecclesiastes 3:12
Psalm 35: 9

DEAR GOD,

thank you for today
as you have saved me from myself
walking in the deluded way.
Dear God,
thank you for today
with all the blessings I see
and the infinite blessings I don't.
Dear God,
thank you for today
this moment and every day
I get to walk with you and for you
my Lord, Leader, and Guide.

       Thank you, Jesus, for everything.

THE APOLOGY

Dear God,
I know things I have done were not all for thee.
I know that through those times,
your love encompassed me.
And though I did not deserve it,
your love was still there.
And though I have hurt your son
you have still made me an heir.

While I cannot make any excuses,
I know I have done wrong.
I cannot believe you have stayed with me
and waited this long.

Though I have walked the wrong way
and lived my life wrong,
There is one thing I can say
and it feels good too:
I apologize,
and thanks for helping me through.

DEAR ANYONE,

If you feel as though
I have ever emotionally harmed you,
in any way, shape, or form.
I apologize
I truly am sorry.
Please, please, please
forgive me.
While it is not for me, I would not know.
I am the nobody you will finally get to let go!
Unless your self-image uses the pain
and the struggle.
Remember forgiveness doesn't mean
suppress, forget, or condone.
Please forgive me so you can let go
of bad emotions from believed transgression
holding you away from the Joy.
That which, I'm hoping you will search for
with Jesus Christ's forgiveness today.

FORGIVENESS

The human aspiration should be to be strong in Christ and forgive. For me not to forgive, would cause unbearable emotional pain, anger, & resentment.
Forgiveness does not

**mean to forget
suppress or condone.**

Forgiveness helps with the letting go of bad emotions that come from transgressions and sinful behavior. Forgiveness, in and of itself,
**must also help to slow or stop
the generational passing down of abuse.**

Everyone has something to forgive, please do forgive, and travel to a state of contentment.
Contentment is a State where happiness, love & joy reside.

A TRUE LOOK AT THE GIFTS

Love the lord your God with all your heart and mind.
Put all of your faith in him
as if you were blind.
He giveth many blessings
like the ability to see, hear, walk, talk
and, of course, use your mind.

Why worry about the little things?
like that next payment.
When God has given us the gift of life
and for this gift we do not pay rent?
God has provided for all our basic needs.
So let him know we cherish his gifts
through all of our joyful deeds.

And if we look closely,
this I am sure we will find:
God is the greatest,
so we love him with all our heart and mind.

A 'NEW DAY

When we wake up in the morning
to start a new day.
When all the stress and worry
of the hustle and bustle come our way.
We must remember the glory of God
to give us strength right away.
For our worries are none
if we let God lead the way.
We must throw our problems off
count our blessings, ok.
and always remember
when we start our day:
to pray

<u>a little ditty</u>

I will not fret
I will not frown
I will not cry
For: **Heaven** is
abound.

A QUESTION?

<u>Who am I</u>,
that God would send
his only begotten Son
to suffer on the Cross
for my sins and transgressions?
<u>Who am I</u>,
that God would work
directly and personally with me
even sending a comforting Counselor?
<u>I am</u> the blessed one,
reading this
as my Lord and Savior, Jesus Christ
is always with me,
including while I read this.

Thank you, Jesus.

QUESTION

If there was a Big Bang
and no one was around to hear it.
Why would they call it a theory?
Then, preach it in schools!
We have a similar theory;
but because the singular cause
of all things to come from
nothing is God,
they will not address our theory.
It does not prove their theory
by mandating an exclusion.
It merely proves God is

A SLOW DESCENT...

Upon realizing the feeling of having a bad day,
I sorted through memories of days gone by.
Knowing that much worse days concerning
health and money, gave much better feelings.
On those days I relied solely on Christ.
Upon realizing the feeling of having a bad day,
I realized the truth,
I was simply walking the wrong way!!
I must always first pray for Christ to show me the way
& grant me the feelings of such a day.

THE REVOCATION OF GOD'S PROMISE

I was not forsaken by God.
God was abandoned by me.
I was interpreting, the important question of why?
& using excuses that Man and the Devil
did so intentionally provide.
Causing, the painful plight
of the non-believer that was I.
I did get the privilege to accept Jesus Christ as my Lord and Savior.
Now, I am aware of some of God's gifts,
& God's forgiveness still makes me cry.

BLESSED,

but don't even know it.

Many are blessed, but
do not even know it.
If they had my life, my struggles,
& my worries
maybe they would see!
Well, upon further reflection
and further understanding
I realized the truth.
The sin was envy
for which I must repent and recognize
the one that was blessed,
but did not even know it
was me!
Thank you, Jesus
for yet again, helping me see

GLUTTONY

With gluttony as your friend
the future is craving to no end
and the rationalization to eagerly defend
the sins and transgressions that will eventually happen!
I pray that gluttony will never
seek me as friend and the Holy Ghost
be with me. So, my eyes may see to prevent
the problems caused by gluttony including
all the steps down the path therein.

1 Corinthians 6:19-20

HATE IS UGLY IN ANY COLOR!

Don't let Hate
be your pursuit,
lest happiness
be your enemy &
fear and anger
become your best friends.

What is Prejudice
but a lie caused by the eye
in which Satan must boast
as some humans comply
to the fear, anger, & hatred
so intentionally caused by the lie.

Contentment is a choice, Hate is a choice
If you choose to blame others,
then you've set your fate.
I blame the Comforting Counselor
for my contentment and pray
everyone would choose contentment
with my hero, Jesus Christ too.

John 13: 34-35

AGAIN

Fear & worry caught me yet, again.
Causing my head to spin,
while trying to smile & grin.
Then praying to be saved from
the fear of a future event
that may or may not even happen.

NOTE TO SELF:
If I'm reading this while worrying,
quit! Start counting the true gifts
for something to think about; as not
everyone can see, hear, walk, talk &
fully use their mind.

Luke 12:25

I QUIT!

I just quit. I'm finished with it,
as far as the reoccurring worries over problems in life.
I'm done!
My true need is to continuously secure my walk
with Christ is my absolute best, and pray about it.
The problems of life do get addressed
but as far as the feelings of worry
I quit.
I am done worrying about it!

Matthew 6:25-27

WANT FOR WHAT?

Blinded by a perceived need,
wishing for something
I have not,
Further encumbered
with a seed
that may include envy
and/or greed.

Today, and at least
a little every day,
I choose to be thankful,
giving thanks to God
for the infinite known
& unknown blessings
that I have received.

Matthew 6:19-24

RED ROSE DISTRACTIONS

Roses are red violets are blue
If you pray for a bed of Roses
Please oh please do not complain
because they, may, have,
a few thorns too.

Philippians 4:6-7

MY LIFE IS GOOD, MY LIFE IS GREAT.

Say it again:
My life is good, my life is great!
Break out into a smile and grin.
Let the devil know your happy again.
I know this; I can see, and I can walk & I do it every day.
Thinking about how much fun life would be without those blessings
gives me strength as my terrible definitions of what problems **are**,
loses its strength right away.
I know this I am blessed beyond all reason
as are the ones missing a blessing.
While, my heart and my prayers go out for you.
Know this; you are blessed beyond all reason too.

Philippians 4:19

TRUE RICHNESS

Richness is not a state of monetary wealth
it's a state of mind.
Whereas, envy would be a cause
of its great demise.
For me, true richness
is a state of contentment
with Jesus Christ as
my Lord, Leader, and Guide.

>Faith
>is blind
>known as trust.
>It gives us peace of mind
>further freeing
>us.

Matthew 6: 19- 24 (NIV)

ANOTHER BURDENSOME TASK!

Everything is not; a burdensome task!
Unless you choose it to be.
For the complaints of one
are the blessings of another.
Please, please, oh can't you <u>see</u>?
That was a rhetorical question.

Struggle as I may.
Struggle as I might.
Finding the blessings
in everything is the
way to fight the
believed stressful life plight
and with Jesus Christ to help
make my mind **right**.

THE APOLOGY, AS LEGAL DOCUMENT

Dear God,
I know things I have done were not all for thee.
I know that through those times,
your love encompassed me.
even though I did not deserve it,
your love was still there.
even though I have hurt **Jesus Christ**
your only begotten son
You have still made me an heir!

While I cannot make any excuses,
I know I have done wrong.
I cannot believe you have granted me a stay,
and waited this long.
There is one thing I can say
and further attest to:
I apologize,
and Thanks for helping me,
through everything.

Enacted by:

_____
Name DATE:

Subscribed and Sworn before me
This __day of_____202_   Notary Public

THE PLEDGE OF ALLEGIANCE

I pledge allegiance to the one and only God of all time and space.
My life & this Earth God provided for me, a sinner.
I must stand-up, rejoice, and make known that God's law is the law.
I must state and affirm clearly that my God reigns over <u>all</u>.
Yes, my God reigns!!!

My God provides for me each day my daily bread
and causes me to forgive those who trespass against me
as my God forgave me, a sinner.
We [The Christians] must at all times give our God praise while openly,
without fear of others' personal judgments,
making known what our God hath done for us.
& we all say

Thank you, Jesus.

DECLARATION OF INDEPENDENCE

1. I am a sentient soul; the body is the temple.
   The body is not my property,
   it is my responsibility.

2. I denounce the unhealthy desires of the flesh
   realizing the strength of the stress of wanting
   & give the energy back to the imagination.
   Walk by the Spirit, and not gratify unhealthy desires.

3. I will not hold onto any **bad thing**,
   that I perceived happened.
   I will loose the energy ever given to the **bad thing**
   through forgiveness.

4. My conscience is clear as Jesus Christ paid for all of my sins
   and forgave me too. My conscience is made new.

1. 1 Corinthians 6:19
2. *Galatians 5:16 &* Matthew 6:25-34
3. Colossians 3:13
4. 1 Corinthians 4:4

POOR SOULS

For the lost souls suffering,
seeking to be less lonely,
searching for true meaning,
I have the Cure.
The Cure is Jesus Christ.
I may not know how to adequately deliver this message,
while I wish to not send you running from my Lord,
I am perfectly fine with being uncool for Christ.
The obligation to influence you, as I am able,
my God demands of me.
If you accept the salvation
& repent of your sins,
the eternal life with us to heaven begins.

KNOWING

In this ever-changing world,
In this ever-changing day,
we must find it in our hearts
to love ourselves
as well as those who go astray.
If we do not learn to love our neighbors
and watch what we do and say,
We need not wait for the glory
of the coming Judgment Day.

Every moment in life is a gift from God;
We should cherish every day.
We must all learn to count our blessing,
as the Bible does say
because every day that we stress over money
and make a big fuss,
The devil is watching
and smiling at us.

Matthew 7: 15-23

THERE IS NO EXCUSE

It is not O.K. if I walk a little
the wrong way today,
for what then would tomorrow bring?

No, it is not O.K. if We the Christians
slide a little the wrong way today
for what then would tomorrow bring
for the nation originally under God's favor?

Degradation of the church influence,
increases in violence, trespass, and pollution.
A perceived need for an increase in Mans' laws to protect us
from the evil that resides within Men.

Now, I must reassert, it is not O.K.
If I walk a little the wrong way today!!!

Romans 1: 21 ,22

THE TIME

In a time when the general population
seeks Jesus Christ and fellowship, not.
The understood goal of distraction,
is in the plot,
against our Christian values.
That which the devil doth wish to rot.

I want to be a rebel,
a rebel for Christ.
I want to be a rebel
a rebel for Christ.
Curse me, taunt me, condemn me thrice
I just want to rebel.
Let us all rebel
Rebel for Christ!

They say there is a division of Church and State
that's a lie I state.
The comforting Counselor doesn't leave me at the gate.
I want a license, a certificate, a decree.
I can see, hear, and talk to the lady
across the desk from me.
These are all gifts from God, can't you <u>SEE</u>

WE THE CHRISTIANS

We the Christians must show the way
by completely loving the Lord our God with
all our **heart,**
all our **soul, all** our **strength,** and
all our **mind**
as the Bible does say.
Plus, by loving our neighbors and
forgiving other's sins
our Father in heaven will see
and non-believers will truly see
how We the Christians desire to be.
We must absolutely show the way today, tomorrow,
and every day of this life.

In life the inner peace and joy
that God gives
is meant for every soul that
in this world lives.
We the Christians must show the light
that is brighter than the sun
showing that being a Christian
is enjoyable and fun.
Together we will bring our friends,
our families, and our neighbors with us to Heaven
where we all truly belong.

[sidebar:] [37](#)Jesus replied: 'Love the Lord your God with all your heart and with all your soul and with all your mind.'

I WILL NOT DIE!!!

While, I do not have the answers tonight.
I do have a Bible to help me
walk in the light.

And Yes! when the body dies
the soul flies.
With Christ as my savior,
to Heaven I will rise.

I hope, and I pray,
That we will all make it that way.

Know this: WE WILL NOT DIE!!!
So, let us rejoice so much that
non-believers
will continually wonder, why???

                                                         2 Corinthians 5:8

NOT DEAD YET

A mere moment in time is this life.
For that I must rejoice in the body my God made for me.
Pronouncing the Glory of God for all to see.
Rejoicing as the comforting Counselor lives with me.
When the body dies mourn me not, because in heaven, I will see
Jesus Christ, Christian friends, and family.
If your sorrow is for the loss of me
remember this life is a mere moment in time.
Heaven is an eternity and you, my friend
again, I will see.

2 Corinthians 5:8

www.ingramcontent.com/pod-product-compliance
Lightning Source LLC
LaVergne TN
LVHW051226070526
838200LV00057B/4631